The Women of Candelaria

Mary Richardson Miller

The Women of Candelaria

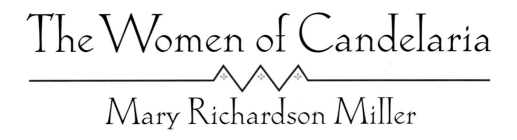

Mary Richardson Miller

Pomegranate Artbooks ✤ San Francisco

Published by Pomegranate Artbooks
Box 6099, Rohnert Park, California 94927

Pomegranate Europe Ltd.
Fullbridge House, Fullbridge
Maldon, Essex CM9 7LE, England

Pomegranate Catalog No. A850

Library of Congress Cataloging-in-Publication Data

Miller, Mary Richardson. 1937–
    The Women of Candelaria / Mary Richardson Miller. — 1st ed.
        p.   cm.
    ISBN 0-7649-0005-6 (pbk.)
    1. Women — Guatemala — Candelaria.   2. Women —
Guatemala — Candelaria — Portraits.   I. Title.
HQ1480.C36M54   1996
305.4'097281 — dc20   96-26463
                                                                    CIP

Designed by Riba Taylor

Printed in Korea
01 00 99 98 97 96   6 5 4 3 2 1

First Edition

Contents

To PAVA,
Programa de Ayuda para los Vecinos del Altiplano,
Chimaltenango, Guatemala,
which introduced me to the Women of Candelaria
and
To the memory of Carmen Torres de Ruiz,
president of PAVA 1986–1990,
and
To the Women of Candelaria
with affection, admiration, and gratitude

Preface

From 1986 to 1993 while my family lived in Guatemala City, I worked for a development organization named Programa de Ayuda para los Vecinos del Altiplano (translation: Development Program for the Neighbors of the Highlands), or PAVA for short. This organization was founded in 1983 to provide relief for victims of the civil war that was ending at that time, a conflict that was particularly devastating to the indigenous population of Guatemala. PAVA's involvement grew from relief to development, helping to rebuild the infrastructure of Indian villages in the highlands that had been destroyed in the war. Later, its work expanded to teaching health education and supporting small business projects, targeting in particular the many women who had been widowed by the war and were left alone to raise their children under the most severe conditions. It was through this organization that I came to know the group of twenty-seven women that I call the Women of Candelaria.

When I joined PAVA in 1987, there were two Home Educators on the staff, young women who taught health education classes to groups of women in highland villages, the majority of whom are illiterate. In addition, the Home Educators taught these women how to run meetings and how to handle monthly food distribution and basic accounting, and shared with them ideas for small home business projects. As liaison between the Home Educators in the field and the board of directors in Guatemala City, I photographed the many activities of the different groups. It was as a result of this work that I met this specific group of women.

In time, the Women of Candelaria came to exemplify for me the endurance, dignity, and courage of indigenous women throughout Guatemala, descendants of the ancient Maya who have retained their language, their customs, and their culture in spite of centuries of repression and prejudice. As I began to know them better, the idea for documenting their daily

lives evolved: to photograph the moments, the colors of everyday life as it is lived in a small country village, focusing on these resilient women, became an irresistible desire for a photography project. Once the women accepted my plan for this venture, I was welcomed into their homes and became a witness to their daily lives.

This book vividly portrays the vital spirit of a specific group of deeply religious women who persevere in spite of repeated setbacks and tragedies such as the recent civil war. As I came to know them and witnessed their daily struggles, I witnessed also their daily triumphs. I want to celebrate these women; I want to honor them.

Mary Richardson Miller

Acknowledgments

My thanks to all those at Pomegranate whose enthusiasm, expertise, and considerable abilities joined to produce *The Women of Candelaria:* Tom Burke, president; Katie Burke, publisher; Jill Anderson, managing editor; Riba Taylor, designer; and Mark Chambers, copy editor. For his encouragement, I wish to thank my agent, Jacques de Spoelberch, champion of *The Women of Candelaria* from the beginning, as was my husband, George Miller, who read the text with attention and care. To all of them goes my gratitude.

Introduction

In the highlands of Guatemala there is a dirt and stone road that runs from the pueblo of San Martin Jilotepeque to the village of Candelaria. The road is wide but rough, and no bus travels there. On either side of this lone access are wide vistas of rolling hills, steep canyons, oak and pine forests, and, in the distance, majestic volcanoes. It is here, in small houses made of earth and raw pine surrounded by fields of corn and beans, that the Women of Candelaria live with their families.

The powerful beauty of the village is in sharp contrast to the brutal work necessary to survive there; not one family owns a horse or a mule, much less a truck; to transport produce to market or visit a health clinic, the villagers must walk to their pueblo, a two-hour trip each way. There is no electricity here, no running water, no machinery of any kind. Only hand tools are used: the hoe, the machete, the pick. Located in the temperate zone of Guatemala's highlands, Candelaria has only two seasons a year, rainy and dry. The focus of the sixty-five families who live there is agrarian, specifically, the family milpas, the cornfields that do not sustain them. Although the families own their land, they do not own enough to support themselves, and in spite of unending labor, the majority remain very poor. For the Women of Candelaria, daily life is a daily struggle to survive.

By nature of their gender, the Women of Candelaria are symbols of intuition, intimacy, nurturing, the humanizers and heart of the community. They have to be strong, to persevere like stalks of corn in a good growing season, and they teach their children to do the same. They know too well the history of the oppression of their people, the Cakchiquel, one of the great tribes of the ancient Maya from whom they descend. Their history before the Spanish Conquest is unknown to many of them yet mysteriously alive in them, affirmed by the cloth they weave, the patterns and symbols learned from their mothers and grandmothers and all the generations before them—each woman in that long line forging a spiritual chain back to the most ancient times of an ancient race. They weave the rhythms of nature into their blouses, called huipiles: green shoots of new corn, purple of bean blossom, stars in the heavens, arc of rainbow, slash of lightning. Today they weave with threads colored not with natural dyes but with vibrant synthetics—glowing pinks, hot oranges, cadmium yellows, reds, and magentas on a field of deep purple or deep blue—colors that echo their surroundings: the sky, the corn, the wildflowers. As they weave the threads into cloth, they weave as well their sacred roots developed over millennia and to this day undaunted by the forced adoption of foreign saints who now collaborate with their ancient gods. These sacred roots entwine not only every thread but every act throughout the day, reinforcing bonds from ancient times.

The Women of Candelaria are a group of twenty-seven, ranging in age from sixteen to forty-four, years that span a particularly tumultuous period in the history of Guatemala. In 1976 an earthquake claimed the lives of more than 27,000 people throughout the country, among them family members of these women. Before the country could recover from that disaster a brutal civil war, long in developing, erupted; the death toll exceeded 100,000 dead or "disappeared" and produced nearly a million refugees. Candelaria was one of the areas hardest hit; all the families there were affected. Too terrified to remain in their houses, where they were prey to both government and guerrilla forces, many families lived in the woods, some for more than a year, eating roots, wild fruit, leaves, and any animal or bird they could kill. Other families fled the area entirely, not returning to Candelaria until a cautious peace was observed by both factions in 1983. In 1985 the first democratically elected president in the history of Guatemala was elected; more recently, the election and forced resignation of a second president was realized without bloodshed. Most important was the awarding of the Nobel Peace Prize to

Rigoberta Menchú, a thirty-year-old Guatemalan woman of the Quiche-Maya. The world's recognition of her fight for justice for all indigenous peoples throughout the Americas has inspired much hope. Today, however, a formal peace treaty still has not been signed.

The daily life of the Women of Candelaria finds its counterparts all over the world in places where an agrarian way of life prevails and ancient methods of farming still exist. The daily acts of each of these women are performed in a long, steady motion beginning at daybreak and ending in candlelight late at night. At this latitude the sun rises abruptly around six A.M.; there is no gradual dawning of light, only the sun's sudden appearance. The woman of the household is the first to wake, in the dark around five, to rise quickly and stir into action the fading embers of the slow-burning night fire so that she can prepare the family's breakfast. Her husband will eat first—hot sweetened coffee and tortillas. At first light he leaves to work in the fields, where all his labor submits to the demands of the seasons: the clearing of harvested fields, the long, meticulous preparation for planting, the labor of the final

harvest. She stirs corn kernels that have been soaking overnight in water laced with lime so that they will be soft enough to be ground at the mill later in the morning. She stirs also the *frijoles* (beans) that have been slowly cooking on a wood fire all through the night for the midday meal.

After her husband leaves for work, she wakes the children, feeds them breakfast, and sends the older ones off to school. Then she and the younger children feed the family's chickens and smaller animals, wash the dishes, and sweep the hard-packed clay floor of the house. She will make numerous trips to the well, usually with a baby tied to her back and often pregnant with another, carrying the weight of a filled *tinaja* on her head—carrying a burden more suited for a draft animal. She must also search for firewood to be cut and hauled home, also on top of her head, and find time as well to go to the nearest water source to wash the family's laundry. Later she walks to the mill with her smaller children, the plastic pan of wet, bloated corn kernels balanced on her head, greeting other women as she goes. This daily ritual is a time to talk of mutual concerns and exchange gossip; the hammering noise of the mill wheel causes the women to lean closely toward one another to catch the news. The mill grinds the corn into *masa*, the dough used in making tortillas.

As the day progresses toward the midday meal, the sound coming from every household is the rhythmic slap-slapping of women making tortillas—enough to last through three daily meals, approximately twenty tortillas for every member of the household. Lunch is the largest meal of the day and the high point—a time to rest and replenish the body and spirit for all except the women, who must continue to work until everyone is fed; only then is it their turn. When a man comes home for the midday meal, it is time for him to rest as well; not so his wife. The days of these women are ones of constant motion; there is little time to sit and reflect, to dream. Yet each woman somehow finds rare moments to create a piece of woven cloth, to plant healthy flowers in a rusting tin can, to crochet a border on a baby's diaper.

For the Women of Candelaria and their families, the dominant force of daily life is religion, and

formal worship takes place in the small, yellow church located at the center of the village. The church—a simple, rectangular cement block structure painted the color of pale corn with a tin roof the color of the earth—was the first building to be constructed twenty-five years ago when the villagers bought the land that would become Candelaria. The land previously was part of a large farm where the villagers worked but that they did not own. It was a historic time. They named the village Candelaria in honor of their patron saint, the Virgin of Candelaria, to whom they pray for protection, guidance, and hope. The church was placed on the highest elevation in the village. Following its completion, the village leaders traveled to Guatemala City to buy a statue of the Virgin and carried her home in a pickup truck rented for the occasion. Her spirit and presence continue to be the focus of spiritual life for the majority of people in Candelaria.

Historically for the Maya, religion and land are intimately united, resulting in a deep reverence for all living matter; almost every household has its personal family altar, so entwined is every

daily act with religious observance. Religion is how morale is sustained in the community, how life is transformed from a subsistent level to a living sanctity. Religion is what raises them above the terrors of natural and man-made devastation; it allows them to regain control of their lives after a violent war or earthquake. The villagers are organized into a community at once sacred and secular, committed to the well-being and cooperation of all who worship in this church.

The overseeing of all religious and community needs is the responsibility of the *comité* (called *cofradía* in many communities, equivalent to "brotherhood"), eight men elected by the community for a one-year period. It is one of these men who rings the bell in the small tower beside the church to summon villagers to worship, to announce special feast days and celebrations, and, if necessary, to warn of approaching trouble. Church services are held twice weekly; they are not only a time for worship but also a time to discuss all aspects of the governing of the community, a time to come to consensus. This has been the traditional way of the Cakchiquel for centuries.

There is also a women's committee of eight members who serve for one year. Called *capitanas*, these women are responsible for cleaning the church, preparing the altar with clean linen for weekly services, arranging flowers, replacing candles when necessary, and preparing for certain rituals attached to saints' feast days. These positions are an honor for those elected but entail additional time-consuming duties and financial responsibilities for people whose days are already filled with urgent demands.

The daily lives of the Women of Candelaria adhere to timeless patterns as they perform the acts women all over the world have performed since agrarian life began—Ana pouring mashed beans into a frying pan to heat for our lunch; Saturnina darting from the kitchen to snatch a sprig of purple bougainvillea to adorn the family's only set of tableware; Efraina setting the threads of her loom as she begins to weave a new *huipil;* Leonarda milking one of her cows. While witnessing their daily lives, I was moving at once in ancient and modern time.

Photography is a powerful communicator. It gives people as isolated as the Women of Candelaria and

their families a sense of identity and belonging, an affirmation of existence. To me it was essential that the daily lives of these women be portrayed in a manner that would inspire hope, that the photographs reveal their courage and dignity in a violent culture that too often values them only as a labor force. It was also important that I act as witness only to their observable behavior and actions of daily life, not to attempt an analysis of the unobservable. I accepted the fact that there would always be a certain distance between us; the inner workings of the descendants of this ancient race were not mine to know, a distance I respected.

The Women of Candelaria were eager to cooperate in this exchange. We spoke to one another in Spanish, our second language (their first being Cakchiquel). We met several times to discuss details: when and how often I would visit, whether or not they could obtain approval from their husbands for this unusual venture. We even discussed what kind of film I would use. Once before I had given them black-and-white photographs instead of color; they were polite, but clearly disappointed. To suggest to them, then, that I use black-and-white film for this project

would have been almost as startling as asking them to drain the color out of their weaving.

My visits were scheduled to provide one full day of photographing for each woman and her family, plus additional sessions for special occasions as they occurred throughout the eighteen months of the project: a wedding, the arrival of a new baby, a child's First Communion, the celebration of the Day of the Dead, the feast day of the Virgin of Candelaria. Thanks to the generous loan of a log cabin by the owners of a neighboring farm, I had a place to live and work. There, to my intense pleasure, I was awakened every morning by a chorus of cows, roosters, woodpeckers, and dogs. Having grown up on a farm, I felt completely at home.

As my project involved more than one-third of the inhabitants of the village, making appointments seemed formidable at first; after our initial meetings, word of mouth was our only means of communication. More than once I wondered what I was doing pursuing alone through endless cornfields the path to someone's house—every cornfield, every path identical, my camera equipment becoming heavier the higher the sun rose.

If I was late the women often sent their children to find me and lead me to their house. For a few women, the project became important enough for me to enter their dreams; once when I sought out a particular woman to make an appointment, I was greeted by the words "I knew you were coming today; I dreamt about you last night."

During the eighteen-month period in which I photographed the Women of Candelaria, I often had to balance conflicting images. I had to remind myself that this village, whose landscape at certain times of the year and in a certain golden light looked like Paradise, had, in fact, been the setting for civil war less than ten years ago — its inhabitants terrorized, many of them raped and murdered. As I walked waist deep in the tall bladed grass known as *sacate*, its vibrant greenness punctuated by stalks of wild salmon-colored and white gladioli, or traveled through cool tunnels of tall corn, I had to force myself not to forget at what price this beauty and tentative peace existed, that remnants of war lay just underneath the grass or the corn, the fields, the houses. Often as I walked to someone's house, time seemed to stand still and I became lulled to dreaming at the sight of a long line of Indian women seemingly gliding across a field, with heavy baskets of lunch perfectly balanced on their heads, to join their husbands in the fields; then, I had to remind myself of all the energy expended for each individual here just to stay alive, just to survive. I had to remember the hopes and dreams of the Women of Candelaria for the future of their children: that someday all the energy expended would result in more than just survival, that it would go toward bettering their lives; that their children would not die of malnutrition and respiratory illnesses due to lack of food and medical help; that the skin of their children would not be stained deep brown with frostbite fungus due to lack of firewood and blankets; that their hair would be blue-black rather than reddish brown from lack of protein; that they would not have to quit school to work in the fields just to have enough to eat; that, if they were fortunate enough to own a cow, they would not have to sell all the milk and cream for extra money but could give it to their own children to drink.

As the project progressed, I gave ninety to a hundred photographs to each woman, more than enough to create a record of a day in her life. Through the photographs we began to find the common threads in our lives in spite of obvious cultural differences. The photographs were more than just a gift to those who had given so much to me; they were a bridge between our cultures, across barriers of language, race, history. Together we could talk about our families, share our common concerns for them and discuss our lives as women. The project had now grown into a cross-cultural experience between us.

Through ordinary, daily acts, the Women of Candelaria give meaning to human value, determination, and courage. It was the images of these simple acts that drove me to document their daily lives; it was their enthusiasm for this project that fueled my energy and inspired me to complete it. While working with these remarkable women, I observed their deep reverence for all living matter, the intertwining of their daily acts and daily religious observance practiced for centuries. As descendants of the Maya, an ancient race whose customs have survived centuries of bitter abuse, the Women of Candelaria, with courage and dignity, faith and grace, remain exemplary keepers of sacred tradition.

Ana Jicha

Throughout her life, twenty-five-year-old Ana Jicha has suffered tragic losses, beginning with the death of her mother in the 1976 earthquake and followed soon after by the death of her father. This left Ana and her only sibling, a sister, to be raised by their maternal grandmother. When Ana was fourteen, her grandmother died and the two sisters were moved to the home of their maternal aunt. At that time, Guatemala was engulfed in civil war, and the violence surrounding Candelaria was among the most intense in the country. Ana's sister, too terrified to stay in the village, fled to seek refuge in the capital; she has not been heard from since and is presumed dead. Of her immediate family, Ana is the only survivor.

Tragedy continued to pursue Ana. At sixteen she was raped, resulting in the birth of a daughter, Maria de la Luz—"Mary of the Light"—a name that contrasts sharply with the violence of her conception. Guatemalan society does not value women, whose abuse and violation attract little attention except to stigmatize them. It is not surprising, therefore, that Ana, having already been violated and with no one to protect her, was again raped and once more bore a child, Esvin Jose, now three years old.

Last year Ana married Justiano, a tall, quiet, impoverished man in his late thirties. They are now the parents of a baby girl, Erika Lorena, a happy, adored child who brings light and laughter to their household. Justiano owns no land on which to grow food for his family, so to support them he is forced to work in neighbors' fields for pitiful wages. The five of them are permitted a small living space within his family's compound, a precarious location on a steep bank at the edge of the property, out of sight of the houses of all the other family members. They are shunned by Justiano's family for reasons that Ana would not discuss. I can only speculate that this condition exists because Justiano brought Ana to his family as a single woman with two illegitimate children or, of equal weight in the community, because Ana and Justiano are evangelical in a village that is predominantly and ardently Catholic. Of the sixty-five families in Candelaria, only five are evangelical, a fact that isolates this minority from the community and makes them suspect. They are denied access to the village church, the place where leaders and members of the community meet to worship and to discuss and deliberate on village affairs. Being shut out of these well-attended twice-weekly meetings is virtually to be in exile in one's own community. Thus, Ana and Justiano are doubly isolated.

While I was photographing Ana
and her family, a small portable
radio was playing, tuned to an
evangelical broadcast originating
in California and transmitted
through Guatemala City. As we
listened to the minister speak—in
soft, soothing tones full of promise, encouragement, and gentle
admonition—it was not difficult
to understand the family's attrac-
tion to this religion. The
program's background music was
equally soothing, providing
comfort for Ana, whose life has
been filled with so much loss and
abuse. As a woman in this culture, she is not permitted to give
voice to all that has happened in
her life; she cannot express her
anguish, her suffering. Her pain
is silent, but her religion offers
hope and promise in a life other-
wise bereft of those expectations.

Cirila Camey

Cirila Camey represents the older generation in the PAVA group. Daily she oversees a household of fourteen people, a small community consisting of twelve children—four sons and eight daughters—and her authoritative husband, Eduardo Garcia. Cirila, at forty, is still able to give birth, but her body is weakening; she spent two months in the hospital in order to have her most recent baby. Her husband, at fifty-five, shows the strain of supporting his large family on land that will not be sufficient in the future for the livelihoods of the sons who will inherit it.

Cirila's household is run with strict precision. So exacting is the formula for survival for this large family that, as with the building of a pyramid, one omission can mean collapse. Each child knows exactly what his or her duties are. As soon as school-aged children return home, the boys go to the fields, the girls to their chores in the house; all the able-bodied older children watch over the younger ones. A large mound of *masa* is mixed and kneaded daily to form the 280 tortillas needed to feed the family. The dough is patted into shape by Cirila and at least three daughters; the rhythmic slap-slapping is at once urgent and comforting. Laundry for fourteen is done daily, an enormous labor in which clothing is beaten on large, flat rocks in a stream that parallels the road in front of the family's house. It is then rinsed in shallow water, which is low at this arid time of year, and hung to dry on the neatly stacked woodpile.

No matter how demanding is Cirila's own daily schedule, this deeply religious woman is grounded in faith and compassion for the suffering of all living beings. Once I saw her take a neighbor's dying child, suffering from severe malnutrition, to a PAVA food distribution. Even though Cirila has her many children to care for, she wants to help others all she can.

Having themselves received no education, Cirila and her husband have worked hard to ensure that their children are not thus deprived. Their daughter Saturnina, one of the younger members of the PAVA group, completed her primary education, which is nothing short of miraculous in a family plagued by so many demands just to survive. Cirila, devout in her belief in a powerful God, ancient gods, and compassionate saints—and doing her part on earth to aid them all—considers the sight of a daughter's diploma hanging on an adobe wall to be her reward.

Dora Marroquin

∧∧∧∧∧∧∧∧∧∧∧∧

Dora Marroquin was born near Candelaria on a neighboring farm, Las Mercedes. Of their nine children, her parents were able to educate only the two sons. The seven daughters, including Dora, received no education at all. She now gamely attends literacy courses with encouragement from her two school-aged daughters. Dora, however, doubts if she can continue. "I cannot get my brain to work," she says. "I get so nervous trying to learn." Her words underscore the heroic effort required to develop a mind that has never been schooled.

Dora is the only member of the women's group born of European stock. Although she regularly attends the women's meetings, she is a silent participant, always in the background; she becomes animated only at home with her family. She and her daughters do not wear the traditional dress of Candelaria, nor do they weave. Her husband, Fidel Mateo, does

not allow Dora to work in the fields like the majority of women in Candelaria, implying that it is too menial for his wife.

Excitement is evident when I arrive to spend the day with this family. Dora has arranged a beautiful bouquet of zinnias, hibiscus, and marigolds to welcome me, and her children are eager to be photographed holding it. Dora and the children take me on a tour of their house to see the bedroom, with beds covered with gay yellow bedspreads; the stuffed animals (the first such toys I've seen in Candelaria), which the children show me with pride; and the tiny kitchen, large enough only for Dora and one child to help her. We walk out past the family's fields, now being cleared by Dora's husband for planting. Dora proudly points to the family's healthy animals: an oversized sow soon to produce a large litter, a cow and her calf, and chickens in an active henhouse.

The family's land is sufficient to support the family now, but Dora is pregnant with her sixth child. Is the acreage adequate for the future of this family? Will the daughters be able to finish their basic education? Will the sons be able to attend school, or will education be sacrificed, as it was for their parents, to help a large family survive?

The beautiful bouquet arranged in the morning was somehow still fresh in the afternoon as Dora and I discussed the precariousness of her family's future. The endurance of the flowers seemed to underscore the endurance of Dora—like the blooms of the bouquet, endeavoring to live and to hope.

The Women of Candelaria

Efraina Salazar

To enter the house of thirty-nine-year-old Efraina Salazar is to experience an atmosphere of harmony and order rarely seen in Candelaria, where the lives of women are often overwhelmed by the work of raising large families. Due to an emergency hysterectomy, Efraina, the mother of four daughters, can bear no more children and thus has lost the dream of producing a son, which is a great sorrow to her. Although she acknowledges that having fewer children allows her the time to attend literacy classes, to serve as *capitana* in the church, and, perhaps, to enjoy more robust health, her failure to produce a son weighs on her heavily. She lives in a culture that holds women responsible for the gender of their babies, that values sons more than daughters.

A devout woman, Efraina does not brood. She is proud of her daughters, who all encourage their mother's brave attempts to become literate and who, unlike her, will all receive diplomas from Candelaria's primary school. On the day of my visit, Efraina's household was in a holiday state, her daughters' excited laughter filling the air, a litter of kittens playing underfoot, and our lunch simmering on the stove. Efraina was eager to start weaving a new *huipil,* and she and three of her daughters hurried through the morning's chores: washing breakfast dishes, sweeping the clay yard, and hanging wet laundry to dry on tree branches, fence posts, and the tile roof of the house.

As her daughters assembled the necessary materials to begin the new weaving project, Efraina knelt on the hard-packed clay of the yard and began to prepare the backstrap loom. With one end of the loom tied firmly to a tree, she placed the other end—a wide leather band—around the lower part of her back; holding the assemblage taut, she then began to separate the long strands of black thread that would form the background for the designs. She explained that a new *huipil* is always begun with a prayer for the strength and patience to weave beautiful cloth, an intricate process that often takes months to complete, demanding concentration and skill. Her daughters are learning from her, just as Efraina learned from her own mother, each generation learning from the preceding one for centuries. This living, ancient art is threatened today by modern technology; elaborate machine-embroidered blouses like the ones worn by Efraina's daughters are slowly replacing handwoven ones. We spoke of this as we sat talking while Efraina's two younger daughters wound thread into large balls, the oldest one weaving next to her mother, and the kittens continued to cause kitten-chaos the rest of the afternoon.

Emiliana Luch

Upon my arrival, it was clear that I would have a difficult time focusing on Emiliana Luch, a gentle, withdrawn woman whose demeanor was in stark contrast to her irrepressible, excited daughters, Maria Cecilia and Antoinetta, and her husband, Balbino; so eager were they to begin photographing, so undesirous was she. Although welcoming in her timid manner, this unusual day was clearly a strain for Emiliana, and her husband, aware of this, stayed close to her, coaxing and protective.

Once Emiliana felt certain her daughters were suitably dressed and our initial photographs were completed, Emiliana was anxious to return to her smoke-filled kitchen. There she stayed until the end of the day, working with her mother and sister, who had walked a long way from a distant village to help Emiliana cook for this occasion. Her relatives greeted me with reluctance, their manner unfriendly and suspicious, refusing to join the family for photographs; the encounter was a rare instance of hostility. Their suspicious manner suggested a fear of photographs or of foreigners, or, because of the recent violence and civil war, a fear of strangers. I will never know, and Emiliana's manner did not invite disclosures. She was like a frightened deer who I was afraid would bolt at any moment.

It was Emiliana's husband who directed his family to pose in various places for photographs, and it was he who sat and talked with me about the daily lives of his family. He had worked hard to prepare for this day, going out early in the morning to gather wildflowers to decorate an altar that he had assembled with holy pictures and a table borrowed from a more prosperous brother who lived nearby. He arranged the flowers in an empty powdered milk can, the effect so dramatic that it reduced his two daughters to rare silence when they entered the only room of the tiny adobe house. He also picked enough gladioli and rose mallow to use as props in pictures of his wife and daughters and posed them with the oranges I had brought as a gift. More than any other husband in the women's group, Balbino clearly relished this day; he had even stayed home from working in his fields. He and his daughters treated the day like a rare and joyful gift, and so it was for us all, except for the one person I had wanted to focus on. Possibly, Emiliana said more by her withdrawal from the activity of her husband and daughters than my photographs could ever reveal.

Several weeks later, I returned to Emiliana's house to deliver her photographs. It was midmorning, and I was surprised to find her in bed. Balbino had gone to the south coast to cut sugar cane, and the children were off playing with their cousins. Emiliana told me that she was sick and that she had left the PAVA women's group. She also said that she did not want to participate any more in the photography project and seemed relieved when I said good-bye. This withdrawn, gentle woman seemed to be withdrawing still further.

Eudiviges Coy

My visit to Eudiviges Coy underscored the hardships on women and their families caused by poor health conditions, the bitter truth of life as lived by the majority of the people of Candelaria and similar villages throughout Guatemala. Thirty-five-year-old Eudiviges and her husband, Pedro Camey, have both required hospitalization during the past year. Eudiviges was gravely ill during the birth of the family's only son, one-year-old Jose Pedro. The situation was further complicated by her husband's emergency appendectomy six months later; he is still in pain, making it difficult for him to work.

The bills for the two hospitalizations totaled six thousand *quetzales,* a sum equal to the approximate average annual income for a family in Guatemala. The family has had to sell one-half *manzana* of land, which means less space to plant, less food available for the family, and fewer crops to sell for needed cash; not to have sold their land would have meant the threat of foreclosure. Meanwhile, their oldest child, thirteen-year-old Julieta, had to go to work in the capital to earn extra money for the family, sacrificing the opportunity to graduate from the primary school.

In spite of these setbacks, Eudiviges, a spunky woman with strength and humor, was eager to discuss her family and their lives in Candelaria. Due to a mix-up in communication, she had not expected me the day I arrived, but she gamely went out and killed the first chicken she could catch for our lunch. As she worked, she talked about her health problems and the years of civil war. She pointed to a spot a few feet from where we sat to show me exactly where her sister-in-law had been repeatedly raped by soldiers. The family was so terrified that they fled to the capital, returning after a year only out of fear that their property would be destroyed or confiscated.

Eudiviges's older children work hard to help their parents. Ten-year-old Rosario, although attending school in the morning, is able to help her mother with countless chores, never having to be asked: washing the breakfast dishes, watching over the younger children, running to fetch water from a spring far from the house, feeding the family's livestock, helping to make tortillas—always trying to spare her mother.

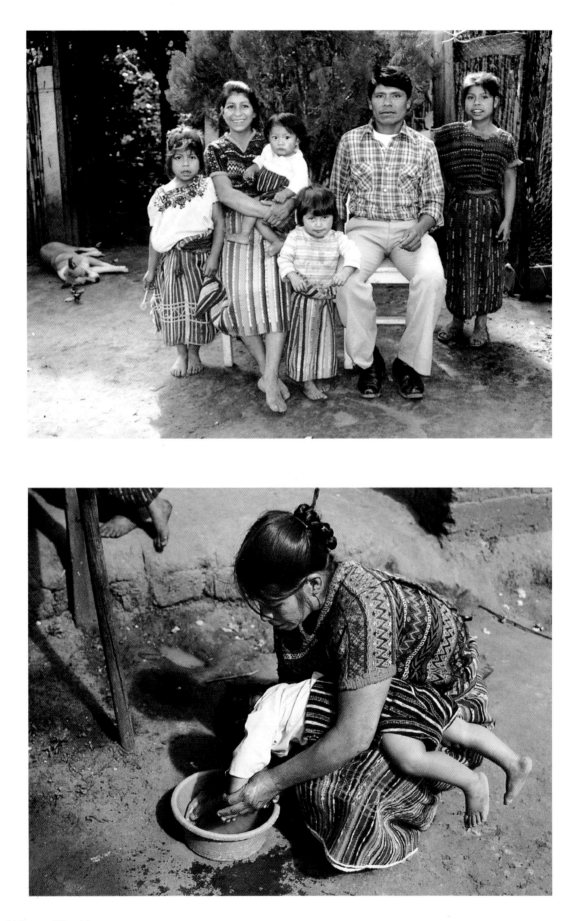

Felipa Pichaya

Crippled by polio at the age of two—her body twisted, her legs weak—twenty-two-year-old Felipa Pichaya struggles to stay upright with the aid of two stout sticks as we walk the long path through the cornfields to her house.

Felipa is the oldest of four children. Her father, an abusive alcoholic, died in 1986; her mother, Juana Coc Chuta, a gentle and bewildered woman, drifted into insanity soon after his death, leaving the burden of supporting the family to Felipa. As the oldest child, crippled or not, she was expected, at age fifteen, to go out and work in the pueblo as a maid. When she left her family's house, her ill mother could not care for the other young children. The two older ones could fend for themselves, but the youngest fared badly, her malnutrition becoming so severe she is now hospitalized for life in an orphanage in Antigua.

Felipa still feels guilty that she was not at home to protect her little sibling and is bitter at the memory of her father, who sold their mother's valuable land to keep himself in drink, forcing the family into poverty. The lost property, a prize piece of woodland bordering a river, was essential to the welfare of the family; considering the difficulty families have obtaining sufficient water and firewood, it is easy to understand her bitterness. Now the children must search for wood far from home and carry water a great distance. Both chores fall to Felipa's brother and sister, now old enough to share equally in running this troubled household.

One of Felipa's greatest pleasures is weaving. In a culture where women generally excel at this ancient craft, Felipa's work is exceptional; with it she can earn extra money. She also loves to embroider and creates her own designs and colors. She takes pride in her work and has the true artist's passion for pattern and color. Whenever possible, she does her handwork outdoors, setting up her loom in the light, surrounded by large clumps of *sacate* and the sound of the doves and chickens she raises to sell, the sadness in her life momentarily forgotten.

Felipa is a devout Catholic, and once a she week makes the laborious journey over rough paths to the village church to worship and to be a part of the community. She says that when she was young, she thought only of herself and nothing of God; now, she says, "It's the opposite. I think only of God and nothing of myself. God has changed my life."

Francisca Garcia

Born in 1970, Francisca Garcia had a childhood branded by Guatemala's civil war. As Candelaria was located in one of the most embattled zones in the country, many villagers fled to other areas. Francisca's family, however, chose to stay, hoping to protect their property and livestock, a decision that forced them into hiding in the woods for more than a year. Caught in the crossfire of the warring factions, Francisca's family eventually lost everything they owned: their houses were burned, their livestock killed or stolen. They were able to survive and sustain morale only by joining forces with other families who had also chosen to remain.

Now, a decade later, Francisca and her family have rebuilt their lives. Francisca completed her primary education and, soon after graduation, married Jose Estuardo Bernardino. They have three children—two daughters, Ana Maria and Claudia Patricia, and a six-month-old son, Andres Estuardo.

Because her husband is a carpenter, Francisca's house is built of broad boards, not the usual adobe; it is located in the middle of a spacious yard high on a hill with views of the village and two volcanoes. Francisca and her husband have planted a lawn, which he keeps trimmed with a machete; together they have planted George Washington orange trees, banana trees, rose bushes, *nísperos* (loquats), and the vines of the pear-shaped *güisquil*. Francisca's need to beautify her surroundings is evident everywhere.

Although naturally reserved, Francisca was the only member of the women's group to express curiosity about life beyond her village and country. She specifically wanted to know about the condition of women and children in the United States, to discuss birth control and the views of the Catholic Church, the expense of raising a family. She and her husband are interested in family planning, but only on their own

terms, those that respect the traditions and beliefs of their culture. They know that having too many children overtaxes their land, food supplies, and health, but centuries of tradition and belief dedicated to life, family, and reverence for the growing forces of the earth do not easily accept the idea of limiting life.

After lunch Francisca, with baby Estuardo tied securely on her back, walked to the fields with her two daughters to help her husband with the planting. The little girls were taught how to plant beans evenly between the shoots of young corn. Their father bored a hole in the damp earth with a long sharpened pole, and the little girls placed three black beans in every hole. There is a unity in this family that is impressive, a harmony among the family members that bodes well for their future.

Graciela Quevedo

When the mother of a family dies in the highland culture of Guatemala, the eldest daughter is immediately cast into the role of surrogate mother. Graciela Quevedo inherited this legacy at seventeen when her mother died of cancer soon after the birth of her seventh child. Graciela's maternal grandparents, who lived on adjoining property, decided to raise the baby, knowing that Graciela would have enough work taking care of her father and five siblings. The immediate consequence was that Graciela could not complete her schooling, already interrupted once when the family fled from Candelaria for a year at the height of the civil war. To complete her final year and receive a diploma was now out of the question. Her attitude about this dead dream, however, is one of acceptance and cheerful resignation: this is the way life is, and this is her duty.

Three years after the death of her mother, Graciela's father was killed. He was shot while working in his fields—a case of mistaken identity in a vengeance matter. The despair caused by this second death caused two of Graciela's siblings to leave the village, to risk the overland trip to California to look for work and a less violent way of life. Other siblings want to follow; Graciela does not. As difficult as her life is, she is at home; she uses the Spanish word *querencia*, which means "the place where one belongs."

Graciela was born a blend of the two conflicting cultures that live uneasily together in Guatemala: her mother was a descendant of the ancient Maya tribe the Cakchiquel, her father of colonial Spanish stock. Her clothing reflects the uneasy fusion: Graciela wears the loose blouse of the Ladino and the *corte*, or skirt, worn by indigenous women.

One of the most distinguishing characteristics of Graciela is her walk. She walks with purpose, head up, as if she had an appointment with someone. She is treasurer of the PAVA group—very able, always to be counted on, and responsible. She is good with figures and planning, helping to run meetings as well as she organizes her household.

Graciela receives much support and affection from her maternal grandparents, who, at eighty-five, are highly respected as the oldest residents of Candelaria. They speak of the poverty of their childhood, when they lived on wild herbs, roots, and any animal they could catch. Candelaria was then part of a *finca*, or large farm; later it was sold in parcels to the present inhabitants. After a long lifetime of hard work, they are people of property and stature in the village. Their love for their dead daughter's children is strong.

During this project, Graciela's grandfather died suddenly; the family's celebration of the Day of the Dead, which fell one week later, was made more poignant by his absence. The family ardently welcomed his spirit back to his home altar, carrying armloads of flowers from his wife's garden to his grave. The family found itself in union once more with death— a more acceptable death, however, than others in the family.

Isabel Ixcaco

∧∧∧∧∧∧∧∧

While walking the narrow clay paths to the house of Isabel Ixcaco, I followed a line of women carrying on their heads deep baskets packed with lunch for their families working in the fields, far from home. We entered groves of tall pines; their lower branches had been stripped for firewood, and the few branches left at the top made them resemble tall columns topped with plumes. The cool thicket was filled with the song of a *cenote*, the trumpeter bird the ancient Maya called "the bird of four hundred voices" because it mimics so many sounds. It is not easy to find the new adobe and wood house of Isabel and her husband, Vicente Car, so dense and lush is the undergrowth surrounding the family compound. I was glad for the company of these women who guided me.

Isabel's house is surrounded by high hills covered with patchwork fields of corn, beans, and squash, the different plants sown in alternating rows as indigenous

people of the Americas have always sown them. Isabel and Vicente have also planted a variety of fruit trees to supplement their basic diet: oranges, lemons, avocados, *anonas* (custard apples), and *granadillas* (passion fruit); Isabel picked me an armful as a gift to take home.

Though only twenty-six years old, Isabel possesses a strength and dignity beyond her age. Her parents died when she was a small child, and she and her only sibling, a sister, were raised by their grandmother. They never attended school. Isabel has a strongly defined face that is as distinct as those sculpted on ancient Mayan stelae; despite a life of adversity, her eyes are calm. She and Vicente have two sons, four-year-old Carlos and a new baby boy, Roni, six months. Carlos, delighted by the rare occasion to be photographed, wanted an image of himself holding every animal and bird his family owned, and there were many.

I spent considerable time photographing the family and visiting little cousins while the family's large tom turkey presided over the crowded poultry yard. The large bird endured stoically until finally, when freed, he shed every one of his handsome tail feathers, so great was the shock of our attention. Celestina, a little cousin of Isabel's and playmate to Carlos, hoping to be included in photographs, wrapped herself in Isabel's *rebozo* (shawl), in the tradition that would guide her through life, enduring, persevering like her cousin Isabel, the woman who is her mentor.

Juana Lopez

∧∧∧∧∧∧∧∧∧∧∧∧∧∧

Juana de la Rosaria Lopez Salazar and her family represent a growing change in the highland culture of Guatemala. Preferring evangelism, they have rejected the traditional religion of their people, the blending of ancient Mayan beliefs and Catholicism; they refuse, as well, to speak the ancient language of their ancestors, the Cakchiquel, nor do they want to teach it to their children.

Juana, her husband, Jorge Camey Salamon, and their four children are one of the five evangelical families in this traditionally Catholic village. Catholic worship and communal affairs are combined in twice-weekly services, which this family does not attend. They live apart. But Juana, proud of her faith, wears her religion like a banner.

Strength and organization are evident in Juana's family. One feels, as well, that her role as wife and mother is valued; consideration is evident here for her hard work. A well has been dug, centrally located for all the needs in the family compound; next to it are a place to do laundry and another place to wash dishes. All work areas are surrounded by the lush growth of fruits, herbs, and vegetables. Although extremely busy, Juana is spared some of the grinding labor that is the daily routine for the majority of indigenous women in Guatemala.

As the family has more than enough property, Juana does not have to buy corn or search for wood; the family's *milpas* and woodland are sufficient for their needs. Consequently, Juana and her children will not have to travel to the south coast at harvest time when her husband goes to earn extra money; she is relieved, she says, because their children usually sicken in the different climate and in the poor living conditions too often found there for migrant labor. If her husband goes — and he might not, due to a cholera scare — it will not be for survival purposes; rather, it will be to earn extra money, to get ahead a little: to buy another cow, perhaps, warmer blankets for the family, a new sweater for Juana.

Juana wears the traditional dress for women and weaves cloth for *huipiles* for her daughters and for herself. Jorge, however, favors modern Ladino clothing, unlike his father, Sotero, who arrived this day wearing the traditional clothing for males in the area, which now no male under the age of fifty would consider wearing. Father and son pose for a photograph, illustrating this change in tradition: Jorge in typical Ladino clothing, his father in a white shirt, white trousers with a red sash, and a brown-and-tan–checkered woolen apron. Father and son spoke Cakchiquel between themselves but only Spanish when the rest of the family was together. Changes in the culture are evident everywhere.

Leona Esquit

It was harvest time in the highlands when I arrived to visit twenty-six-year-old Leona Esquit, who, ten days after the birth of her fourth child and first son, was shaking the moisture off armloads of *frijoles* before laying them on a large cloth to dry in the sun. Her husband, Ramon Garcia, had been picking them since first light, and the piles were high. The demands of the harvest do not allow time to rest nor ease the workload of a mother who has recently given birth.

As Leona and I spoke together of the role of women in her culture and the changes taking place, her household continued in its customary routine: sweet potatoes and *atol* (a soybean beverage) were cooking on the stove; the new baby was asleep; the cat and her single kitten were napping in a box by the stove; a neighbor came to the door to buy a branch of Leona's eucalyptus tree, the leaves to be boiled down into a medicinal tea; the harvested beans were drying.

As Leona's property is more extensive than the average family's holdings in Candelaria, and because there is income from Ramon's carpentry business plus a market stand they operate in the pueblo twice a week, this hardworking family prospers more than most. They can even afford to hire people to help with the harvest, a rare luxury in Candelaria, where most children are forced to leave school to help their parents at the critical, busy harvest or planting time. There is even occasional help for Leona— twin sisters, daughters of a neighbor. She also has a good husband, she says, who helps her with their children.

Every January for the past fifteen years, Leona Esquit and her family, no matter how small the children, have traveled three hundred kilometers in a packed, lavishly decorated bus to Esquipulas, the home of the Black Christ, the greatest pilgrimage site in Central America. This is a sacred quest, the most

important religious observance besides Easter during the year. Pilgrims, like Leona and her family, arrive bearing their prayers: supplications for health, for the success of their crops, that life will be more tolerable, that pain will be eased, that a son will be born. Did Leona and her husband pray for a son last year? After three daughters it is likely; her obvious joy at the arrival of ten-day-old Pedro, the first son of four children, was appreciable— the necessity of producing a son in this culture is formidable. Her little son flourishes. For Leona and her family, life is good, filled with bright hope for the future.

Leonarda Garcia

Leonarda Garcia, a strong, animated woman, calls herself La Abandonada, the Abandoned One. She says that as a child she was abandoned by her parents, that she never attended school, and that no one has ever helped her in life. Ever.

At forty-one, Leonarda is the widowed mother of eight, the grandmother of three. In a culture where division of labor is strict, the absence of a male head of household is devastating. Who will till the soil now and prepare it for planting? Who will weed the bean plants, the squash? Who will travel to the coast now to earn urgently needed cash during the coffee and sugarcane harvest? Be father to his children? Husband to his wife? Even in households with both marriage partners, each works from earliest dawn until after dark. How can one woman manage alone? But Leonarda has not only managed but managed well. The Abandoned One is a resourceful woman with a shrewd sense of survival.

In a community where high status is accorded to the owner of one cow, Leonarda owns two, each with a newborn calf, plus two heifers born the previous year— livestock that provides ready cash when finances are strained. She also owns three fattening pigs, numerous chickens and turkeys, some cats for mousing, and, a rare extravagance, two bright green pet parakeets whose lively chatter greets all who enter her compound. Leonarda, is, then, a woman of property. She derives her main income by going twice weekly to the market in San Martin Jilotepeque to sell eggs, fresh white cheeses made from the milk of her cows and wrapped securely in a banana leaf, perhaps a chicken or turkey, a fattened pig: whatever she can carry in a basket on her head or drag by rope on the two-hour walk to market. As her house is located beside the only road that leads into the village, Leonarda earns additional income by running a small, profitable store from her kitchen. Throughout the morning there are repeated knocks at her

gate, especially as lunchtime nears: a farmer walks in from the fields where he has been working to buy a dozen tortillas; a neighbor asks to buy a bag of salt. Another neighbor arrives to trade a small branch of eucalyptus, used here medicinally, in exchange for a chili pepper to make a sauce. The ancient barter system persists to this day.

In Candelaria childhood is brief, and all Leonarda's children, in addition to their schooling, have extensive duties to help their mother maintain their household. Even Leonarda's three-year-old son, Jose Domingo, helps out, feeding the family livestock, throwing grain to the poultry, collecting eggs, or carrying dried cornstalks in from the fields. It would be understandable if Leonarda kept her children home from school to help with the hard daily routine, but she is determined that her children will receive what she did not, that they will grow up neither illiterate nor abandoned, and she is succeeding.

Luz Car

Luz Car, the eleventh of thirteen children, is the fifteen-year-old daughter of strictly traditional parents. Though she lacks only the final year needed to complete her basic primary education, her father feels it is more important that she stay home to help her mother care for the family's four cows than that she complete her schooling. His word is law. Her two younger brothers will finish their schooling; a son's education takes precedence over a daughter's. Carrying water and cutting fodder for cows is women's work. The family has four wells and four cows; Luz's future is arranged.

The women in the PAVA group realize the crucial need for education for all their children, but too often the education of young girls is sacrificed ahead of the boys' when family demands are urgent enough to necessitate more helping hands. In the group, only two women out of twenty-seven have completed their primary education. With sadness, Luz accepts her father's decision.

Throughout the day I photographed Luz as she followed her daily routine, in which she demonstrated how capable she was, how responsible toward her duties. She also was very much a fifteen-year-old girl. She giggled a lot, changed her blouse three times, repeatedly disappeared into the house to recomb her hair. When I later returned for a second session to photograph the family altar for the Day of the Dead, a few weeks after she had absorbed the results of the first session, I was startled to see quite a different person waiting to be photographed. Luz had suddenly become very sophisticated: her hair was swept forward over one shoulder, the other side dramatically swept back; her gaze was direct, almost bold. She had a poise, an assurance she had lacked when we first met. She obviously had consumed all manner of information from the first photographs and set about making "improvements." Maybe the appearance of the "new" Luz was too threatening to her father, because after this second session

the family, which had previously been the epitome of warmth and hospitality, never invited me to return and avoided speaking to me when we met on the road.

Photographs reveal and influence, often clarifying moments in life more profoundly than sitter and photographer realize; photographs have the power to inform, to teach—even, in the case of Luz's family, to threaten.

Marcelina Garcia

The approach to Marcelina Garcia's house is a narrow clay path that ascends a long, gently rising hill, continues past two wells shaded by apple trees, and finally arrives at her adobe house located halfway up the hill.

Marcelina Garcia, thirty years old and the mother of five children, was born in Escuintla, on the south coast. There she met her future husband, Marcos, after he and his family moved there to escape the civil war devastating Candelaria during his childhood. Marcelina is a mercurial woman, outspoken and apt to express her feelings freely; she is both peppery and merry, a true contrast to her authoritative but more even-tempered husband.

As her husband is away from home working in the capital twenty-four days of the month, Marcelina fills both parental roles for their five children, one of whom, eight-month-old Ardiana, was born with a severe heart defect. I was not told of this illness on the day of the photographs; I learned of it several months later, when I met Marcelina walking without her baby tied to her back, which for a young mother in this culture is extremely rare. With sadness, she told me that the baby had died, that her survival had depended entirely on a heart transplant, an operation too costly to even be considered. In a country where the infant mortality rate is second only to Haiti's in the Western Hemisphere, and where families like Marcelina's live on less than two thousand dollars a year with little or no access to any form of health care, the hope of such an operation is out of the question, resulting in the fatalistic attitude so often found here in families whose children have died.

Marcelina worked hard to produce a delicious lunch on the day we spent together: a vegetable stew, roast chicken, and tortillas, all cooked on a stove that consisted of three rocks placed on the ground with wood stacked on top, camp-fire style. She had to kneel at this stove to cook. After placing tortillas on the *comal* or stirring the vegetables, she would stand up to get something she needed, then kneel again to reach the stove, kneeling, standing, kneeling, standing, for hours at a time. The only light in the large room entered from the doorway and from two smoke holes in the roof. Her husband, considerate and aware of the tiring situation for his wife, had made plans to build a new kitchen for her; materials were piled up outside the house, and the building was to commence the next day.

Later, when I delivered the family's photographs, Marcelina directed an older child to go fetch the egg basket. As she looked carefully and critically at each photograph, making comments, merrily pointing out details to her equally delighted children, she calmly tossed each photograph over her shoulder into the egg basket without once looking to see where they

landed; she never missed.
Unlike the other women, who
stored their photographs in
boxes, frames, or albums,
Marcelina chose to keep the
documentation of a day in the
life of her family in an egg
basket, underscoring the fact
that Marcelina was a singular
woman who would always do
things her way.

Margarita Bernardino

Wedding preparations were cheerfully under way when I arrived to visit Margarita Bernardino. Her youngest sister was to be married the next day, and several family members, particularly the bride, were eager to perform a "dress rehearsal" for my cameras. For the occasion, Margarita had created a bride's bouquet of wild calla lilies and hibiscus from her own garden, and she was busy braiding broad bands of white silk into the bride's long hair.

Margarita, one of nine children, was born in Candelaria and descends from generations of midwives on her mother's side of the family. The skills of midwives are highly respected in this rural community, and they have been enhanced recently by additional training from UNICEF. This is one of the rare professions to which women can aspire in this culture; it accords Margarita respect and standing within the community.

As I watched Margarita perform her daily tasks, I noted a relaxed elegance in her movements. She is not the typical overworked or overburdened village woman. Margarita is spared many of the harsher jobs by her husband, Elardio, and her mother-in-law, who lives with the family. Margarita and her husband have three small children and expect a fourth in a few months. The family has sufficient land to support them, and Elardio, an able farmer, sells firewood as well to earn extra money.

Margarita and I walked together to the family wells for water past fields of flourishing bean plants and newly sprouted corn planted with almost military precision in the soaked earth. We talked about her dreams for her children, the importance of their education, the difficulty of getting ahead.

Several weeks later, as I walked the slippery clay road to Margarita's house, I saw that the corn had grown tall with the plentiful rains and the land was choked with lavender and the wild marigold called *flores de muerto,* whose presence signals the approach of the second of November, the celebration of the Day of the Dead. Margarita did not expect me that day, did not know that I was coming to make an appointment with her to photograph the family's altar. As I approached her house, I saw Margarita hanging laundry to dry on the thatched roof of the pig pen. Smiling as she walked toward me, she said, "I knew you were coming today; I dreamt about you last night." The impact of photography had worked its communication magic—the power of images and the maker of images to penetrate down deep into dreams.

Margarita Culajay

The approach to the family compound of Margarita Culajay is one of the loveliest in Candelaria. A red clay path that originates in the center of the village proceeds through tall grasses and cool woods where people tether their cows for the day, emerging finally into wide expanses of cornfields *(milpas)* and bean fields belonging to families who live in the area. The corn, tall at this time of year, creates a cool tunnel that leads to Margarita's house, and as one emerges into full sunlight at tunnel's end, the buildings, surrounded by flourishing purple salvia, become visible inside the adobe wall of the compound.

This is Margarita's childhood home. Margarita and her three children returned to live here with her family after her husband was killed by the army in the civil war of the early eighties. Before his death, Margarita and her husband lived in a village ten miles from Candelaria, where their daughter and two sons were born. At that time, the conflict between the Guatemalan army and the guerrilla forces was escalating. Margarita's

husband, falsely accused by the army of sympathizing with the guerrillas, was abducted and was never seen again. Left alone with her three small children, Margarita fled the village, hiding in the forest during the day and traveling the dangerous ten-mile journey at night, carrying and leading the children through one of the most conflicted war zones in the country. That she was successful in safely reaching her family attests to her bravery and her innate resilience.

When I first met Margarita, she stood out among the Women of Candelaria because of her size and her generous smile. She is much taller than the average indigenous woman and more robust, emanating a sense of power and dominance. She managed—in spite of being a single parent and having to do more than her share of daily work—to participate fully in the activities of the women's group, the health and nutrition classes, the sewing lessons. Being a deeply religious woman and known for her community participation, she was elected to serve as a *capitana;* with pleasure

and pride she braids her beautiful blue-black hair with a wide sash of brilliant aqua silk, twists it into a *corona* on top of her head, and wears the official *huipil,* the ceremonial blouse of her office. In addition to her PAVA activities, Margarita has managed to receive training from UNICEF to become a midwife and has delivered five babies, including Medarda Osorio's sixth child and, more recently, the third grandchild of Leonarda Garcia.

Margarita and I discuss the overwhelming problems a widow faces trying to support her family alone while still finding the time to participate in community activities. Through it all, Margarita maintains an infectious sense of humor, which punctuates our conversation, especially when my suggestion of photographic subject matter or location amuses her: photographs with a new piglet, for example, or of her laundry hung out to dry on a cornstalk fence. Nowhere were her amusement and hilarity more evident than on a visit we made to the family's terraced vegetable gardens located on the sides of a

ravine on their property, a canyon so steep that we could not see the bottom. As we descended, Margarita and I struggled to keep up with her mother, who led us with such sure steps that she managed to braid her hair as she continued down the incline almost at a run. We passed trees heavy with fruit but were descending so rapidly that the fruit was a blur and therefore unidentifiable; the weight of my camera bag held on one shoulder made me lopsided, and I was praying just to stay upright. The reward for these efforts was found at the lowest depth, a freshwater spring pushing forcefully up from the soaked earth, a source of family pride — to own land with a spring is a special blessing. We were refreshed by the coolness, the sound of the spring water, and the sight of the calla lilies that thrive in the spongy earth and would be taken to market at week's end along with the vegetables from the terraced gardens. Margarita considered it hilarious that I would take still more photographs while trying to catch my breath, the sound of our joint laughter echoing with such insistence that not even the lush surroundings and heavy air could hush our merriment.

Marta Bernardino

Marta Bernardino, one of Candelaria's three midwives, is the mother of seven children; her husband, Fidel, is a village health promoter and member of the *Comité*, the governing body of the community. Although Marta completed only two years of primary school, as an adult she received basic midwifery training in a program sponsored by UNICEF. Her inherited knowledge and practice, as a sister, daughter, and granddaughter of midwives, is blended with modern medical training and methods designed to assist women in childbirth all over the world; she hopes to pass on this information to her own daughters.

For women living in rural areas of Guatemala, where there are virtually no health facilities, the local midwife is the only help and support available to pregnant women. Due to this acute situation, Guatemala has the highest maternal mortality rate in Central America. At age thirty-three, Marta has successfully delivered thirty babies, but should any of the deliveries be beyond her expertise, the only option is for a family member or friend to walk two hours to the pueblo to seek the help of the town's only ambulance and driver, return to the village to pick up the mother who is laboring to deliver her child, and drive to the nearest hospital in Chimaltenango, a two-hour ride over rough roads.

Fortunately for Marta and the pregnant women who seek her help, emergencies have been rare, and with confidence generated by training and experience, she attends to the many women who seek her services. She ministers, as well, to the traditions of her people, to the customs surrounding childbirth. When a baby is born in Candelaria, for example, it is bathed in specially prepared water boiled with the flower of red geraniums, the herb called *chilco*, and the petals of white roses. Afterward, Marta or a family member ties a red thread around the baby's neck or wrist, usually with a small red pouch attached to hold tiny red beans, or a cross, or a holy medal previously blessed by the priest in the pueblo. The color red is significant—a powerful color to ward off evil spirits and sickness and to protect the baby from misfortune.

Marta is a highly respected and valuable member of the community and is understandably proud to wear the uniform of a midwife. Over the traditional *huipil* and *corte* of the pueblo she wears the plastic apron and sterilized head cloth given to her by UNICEF; near her on the table is the medicine chest that was presented to her at the completion of training. Hanging from the rafters above her head are yellow, white, and black ears of corn, *mazorcas de semilla*—the choicest ears selected by Marta and her husband from this year's harvest—which are prayed over and guarded carefully for the next planting season. Between her professional equipment and the ears of treasured corn, Marta is surrounded by fruitful symbols that describe her life: seed, growth, harvest, and birth.

Medarda Osorio

Medarda Osorio and her ten-day-old baby, warmly wrapped in a cocoon of blankets, are seen here surrounded by the natural materials that symbolize traditional living in this highland culture: raw earth of adobe, raw wood of door and furniture, raw fruit of the *güisquil* vine. Above them hang the *mazorcas de semilla,* the best ears of corn chosen from the recent harvest, sacred seed for the next planting. The majority of houses in Candelaria resemble this one, with its age-old adobe construction that is warm in the rainy season, cool in the dry season, and thick enough to block out sound to ensure privacy. The color, smell, and feel of these houses are those of the earth, reminders of the belief of the ancient Maya—Medarda's ancestors—that the first Maya was made of clay pulled from the earth and modeled by the gods into the form of man. From clay also came the raw material for this ancient method of construction.

Medarda was born thirty-six years ago on a neighboring farm. She was, she says, treated indifferently as a child. She says also that she received no education and no one taught her how to do anything, that she even had to teach herself to weave. Medarda and her husband, Jose, are the parents of six children. They are determined that all of them will receive a primary education. There is a feeling of unity and warm affection in this family as everyone works together at daily tasks. To supplement the family income, Jose has started a successful tree nursery selling coffee and shade trees to neighbors in the village. By producing this extra income at home, he will not have to leave Medarda and their children to go to the south coast to work during the coffee and sugarcane harvest.

As in the majority of households in Candelaria, the swirl of activity in Medarda's day starts before daylight and continues throughout the day, the motion increasing as small barefooted children and flocks of chickens circulate around the yard. Even while she is weaving, an activity Medarda clearly loves, the energy of the living creatures surrounding her never slows. Weaving, however, absorbs Medarda. Her concentration is intense as she kneels to secure more threads into the growing length of cloth, but not so intense that she cannot instruct her children to feed the pigs, rock the baby, check the fire on the hearth, throw corn to the chickens. Once the commands are given, Medarda's attention returns to her weaving; she is completely immersed in an act as absorbing as prayer as she weaves the designs that symbolize the cosmos and the earth. For Medarda, the act of weaving not only affirms her ancient heritage and reverence for life but also allows her a small measure of solitary space and calm.

Medarda was especially anxious to have me photograph the family cow, which had recently borne her first calf, a heifer. The birth of this calf is a significant event, a valuable addition to the family's livestock and one of the rare times in this society that the birth of a female is preferable to that of a male. A cow is an ongoing source of income, providing fresh milk not only for family use but also for sale to neighbors. From the cream Medarda makes delicious white cheeses, which she wraps in fresh banana leaves to sell locally or at the market in the pueblo. But owning a cow means additional work; all members of Medarda's family work together to haul water from a distance for this animal at least three times a day and to cut and carry armloads of *sacate* to her. Watching Medarda and her family care for their cow made me feel as if I were moving in ancient time; this is the way agrarian life has always been.

Monica Garcia

In late January, Monica Garcia was elected *capitana* of the village church for the coming year, her official duties beginning on the feast day of the Virgin of Candelaria, the patron saint of the village. This special day, celebrated every February 2, is the holiest day of the year in Candelaria.

Monica is one of the women responsible for cleaning the church and preparing for this two-day celebration, which includes all-night vigils. It is a deeply religious occasion combining ancient rites and Catholic traditions, ancient gods and Catholic saints. A priest is hired from the large pueblo church in San Martin Jilotepeque to conduct part of the ceremonies. The church is decorated with flowers, its floor is covered in fresh pine needles, and embroidered and handwoven cloths cover the altar. For the children,

a carnival spirit enriches the solemn religious services; there are firecrackers and *bombas*, flags and banners, candies and games. Monica is proud of her role in this sacred celebration.

Several months later, when I visited Monica to photograph her family, it was the height of the dry season and the weather was unusually cold. Fields were being prepared for planting; the dust of the parched earth filled the lungs of the villagers, water was scarce, and there was a lot of illness. Monica had been sick for three months, sick enough to seek help from a neighbor to clean the small two-room house where she lived with her husband and six children. Wanting to conserve her energies, Monica asked her only daughter, six-year-old Teresa, to be my guide and companion on a tour of the family's property. Teresa had the poise of an adult and proudly named every tree,

flower, and vegetable in the garden, pointing with particular pride to her mother's favorites, blood-red roses that were struggling to survive in the dry season, just like her mother.

Monica had become leaner and more worn since I had last seen her, a poignant reminder that a life of marginal existence is a source of unremitting stress; it is so hard for people just to stay alive. Will the descendants of the great Maya someday despair of grinding out subsistence? Or will they endure like Monica, persevere like the corn that continues to grow in fields that have been farmed for millennia, persist like the patterns that women like her have woven for centuries and that continue to live in the art of their textiles, living symbols of an ancient race?

Narcisa Ambrocio

There is a feeling of harmony in Narcisa Ambrocio's house, where she lives with her husband, Jose, their four small children, and Juana Garcia, her mother-in-law. The house, located near the top of a long, gently sloping hill, is new, well organized, and more spacious and airy than most in Candelaria. It has, as well, a sweeping view of the family's large cornfields and the pastures and forests of a neighboring farm, and a full view of the setting sun. As her house is close to the village center, Narcisa can hear the toll of the church bell summoning the community to twice-weekly services, which she attends regularly to worship and at which she performs her duties as recently elected *capitana*.

The harmony one feels in Narcisa's household is due in large part to her husband's steady employment outside the village as a carpenter and woodcutter; these skills raise the family's living standards above minimal levels. Their situation, however, is atypical for the majority of people living in Candelaria, where there are scarce opportunities for employment other than farming or leaving the village for weeks at a time to work on the south coast at harvest times. In addition to his employment, Jose owns his own land and farms corn, beans, and squash to provide the basic diet for his family; because he can provide more abundantly for them, they do not suffer the strains of poverty.

Equally important to the unity of the household is the compatible relationship between Narcisa and her mother-in-law, two women who work together in an amicable manner, sharing the burden of daily tasks. Generously, Juana relieves Narcisa of two of the most demanding: the many daily trips to fetch water, the source of which is far from the house, and the incessant search for firewood, without which one cannot cook. Because of this help, Narcisa is able to tend more efficiently to the needs of her husband and children and the family's livestock, the housecleaning, and the laundry, in addition to her church obligations. Thanks to her mother-in-law, Narcisa has been given the gift of time to pursue enthusiastically two favorite activities: her weaving and her flower garden, the latter protected from scratching hens and swarming chicks by a tall cornstalk fence that Narcisa fortifies daily.

Traditionally, weaving with a backstrap loom is a practical function, producing cloth for family use and ceremonial purposes according to distinctive styles, patterns, and colors. Weaving is time-consuming—the slowest way to create art—but for Narcisa it is a joy. Besides using her loom, she often employs a long, delicate thorn, one of three that she owns, to create a special stitch; these thorns were given to her as a wedding present by her mother-in-law and are hidden safely from her small children, wrapped in a bit of corn husk. Her choice of thread colors reflects the warm hues of her flourishing garden: bright reds of salvia and geranium, pinks of

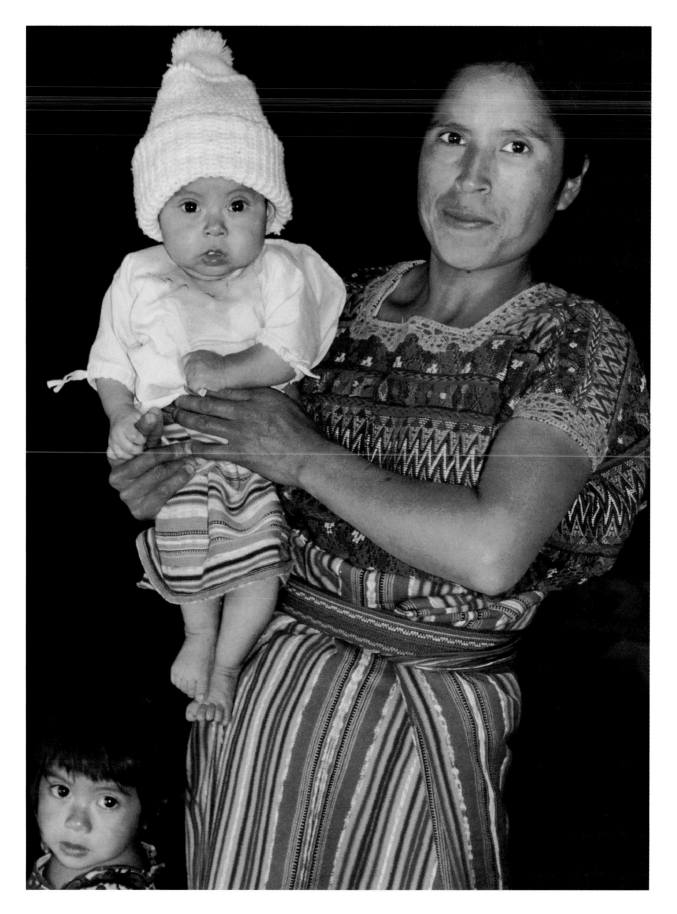

gladiolas and roses, purple of aster, yellow of chrysanthemum, blue of sage, orange of marigold. Weaving in horizontal bands of varying widths, she chooses from the traditional designs of her pueblo, San Martin Jilotepeque, designs such as the jagged arches that appear as slashes of lightning zigzagging across the surface of the cloth, charging the pattern with energy and movement. Other bands are woven in a pattern of small diamonds in colors of pink, purple, blue, and white on a field of green, miniature replicas of Narcisa's garden. Smaller bands of white diamonds on a blue field are stars in a night sky; green diamonds on a purple field are small shoots of new corn after the heavy rains arrive. Stars, corn, and flowers grow according to the seasons, according to the movements and rhythms of the earth. As she weaves the heavens and the earth into her work, she weaves as well her ancient roots, handed down through generations of women like her who practice this living, ancient art.

Olivia Bac

"Hush, Señora, you'll scare the children!" admonished Olivia Bac as I discussed the Guatemalan folktale "La Llorona"—a tale often told to children to make them behave. On this rare occasion, this day of photographs, there would be no place for scary stories, only high excitement at the idea of being photographed. We were seated together in the kitchen talking as Olivia prepared lunch. Her seventh baby, eight-day-old Leticia Roselia, was cocooned in her hammock, hung in the corner of the room. Despite the fact that Olivia had so recently delivered a baby, she showed no obvious sign of weariness; her eyes sparkled, as if her thoughts were only merry ones.

The older children had been allowed to stay home from school that day, and every member of the family had a definite idea about how he or she wanted to be photographed. Because owning animals, especially cows, is a sign of prosperity, all the family's animals were bullied into being part of the photographs. Children and parents wanted photographs first with their cows—with or without their calves—with chickens, with doves, with dogs, even cats. Then siblings supplanted animals; one child wanted a photograph with another child or with parents, in the cornfield, in the barn, in the well-stocked corncrib, always with the admonition to one another: "Don't smile." And then they would laugh.

Surrounded by their children and animals, Olivia and her husband, Benigno Guerra Elias, reveal how they want to be regarded by their community, how they wish to see themselves. The numbers of children reflect their traditional belief in the strength of a large family; the many animals coerced into photographs reflect the relative prosperity of the family; the photographs depicting the filled corncrib indicate a good harvest, critical to survival.

Neither Olivia nor her husband attended school, but literacy is not required to "read" their photographs; these photographs are the storybooks, the folktales of this family—underscoring the power of photographs to communicate through vision a universal language.

Paola Canun

∧∧∧∧∧∧∧∧

Paola Canun has been president of the PAVA women's group since its formation four years ago. Though Paola is uneducated, her natural leadership ability has enabled her to assemble a cohesive body of women who have learned the value of a formal meeting to allow them to speak out on issues that concern them all. This deeply religious woman is also a *capitana* in the village church, an honor, however, that adds extra duties to her demanding daily schedule and additional expenses for her family. For a mother of eleven children to commit herself to these obligations is heroic.

Paola is also tired. The burden of bearing many children is wearing her down, though despite nearly dying from a recent miscarriage, she is, at thirty-five, still able to have more. Like many women in her community, she fears birth control—it is contrary to her religious beliefs—yet she knows well the strain on her health and

is fearful of more pregnancies. Her husband will not consider sterilization for himself or his wife; such an action is too threatening for most men in Guatemala, underscoring the difficulty for women to change their lives. It also reveals the consequences for children in the family, many of whom work as long each day as adults, like Paola's twelve-year-old daughter, Eva, whose help is so vital to her mother she cannot attend school like her siblings; her future is sacrificed.

Paola's life symbolizes the pressing issues and needs of women in this highland culture. The monthly PAVA meetings give them a self-awareness that has never been part of their lives before and has released a courage in them to share their concerns. They discuss illness, the deaths of children, and the prolonged absence of husbands who must seek work outside the village, and they teach each other the medicinal qualities of plants, leaves, and

the bark of various trees, passing on ancient knowledge. At these meetings the need for literacy classes was discussed and acted upon; now classes are held twice weekly in the village church.

The women talk as well about the celebration of ritual in their lives, such as First Communion for their children or the observance of the Day of the Dead. It is significant to Paola and her ten-year-old daughter, Estrella, that these two important occasions coincide on the same day this year and that the spirits of the family's dead members will join her earthly family during the night to celebrate this important rite of passage. Paola's family decorated the altar in their house with *flores de muerto*, spread pine needles to cover the earthen floor, fashioned a cross of marigolds to put on top, and piled offerings of vegetables and fruit on the altar to provide hospitality for the dead and spiritual strength for the living.

Santos Culajay

Although I looked carefully, it was difficult to see Santos Culajay and her small son waiting for me at the top of the steep hill, so lush was the growth of wild and domesticated flowers that bordered the path to the hilltop house where she lived with her in-laws on a farm near Candelaria. I was late. Due to heavy rains, the road had been difficult, and the tall grasses covering it disguised the fact the road was more swamp than thoroughfare. Entering the family compound, where I expected to photograph four or five family members, I was astonished to find fourteen people waiting for me; a cousin had even brought his cow. Such is the excitement engendered by the anticipation of a visiting photographer.

This is a household run by women, Santos and her widowed mother-in-law. As we walked to the distant spring for water, Santos told me that her father-in-law had died the previous year and that her husband can seldom return home, as he does construction work in the capital to support his family. These two women, however, have organized their large household with the same precision women in this culture bring to their intricate, complex weaving, with interdependent tasks set in sequence like a pattern, raising ordinary duties in this household to a higher order.

Dressed in her best for photographs, Santos wore an elaborately embroidered "store-bought" *huipil* and a striped apron made from *tanteros,* colorful cloth used to bundle vegetables at market to carry on women's heads; she showed me her own weaving still on the loom. The combination of these fabrics, part of everyday life here, present a lavish visual feast, as if the myriad patterns found in the heavens and the fields, landscape and cloth, complemented one another, revealing why Guatemalan textiles are among the most prized in the world.

Toward the end of the day, Santos repeatedly requested that I walk some distance to photograph her brother-in-law and what I heard as his *novia,* meaning "girlfriend." It had been an enjoyable day but a long one, so I repeatedly suggested that the *novia* come to the house to be photographed, a response that brought perplexed looks and utter silence to the whole group. Gamely Santos persisted, and by the third or fourth request I exasperatedly declined again and said: "But, Santos, why can't she come here to the house to be photographed?" And Santos, equally exasperated, replied: "But, Señora, she's a cow, and she's tied up in the pasture." I had confused the words for girlfriend *(novia)* and heifer *(novilla),* causing much merriment; surrendering, I walked off with Santos's large family to take final photographs, these last of a young heifer, the pride of her owner.

Saturnina Garcia

Among Saturnina Garcia's possessions, the most important is her framed diploma hanging on the adobe wall of the family bedroom. Saturnina represents the younger generation of women in the PAVA group, and she and her husband, Mario Salazar, are the only couple in the group to have completed their primary education. Both Saturnina, one of twelve children, and her husband, one of eleven, were born of illiterate parents; attaining this basic education reflects the heroic efforts of their families and improves, as well, their chances for a better future.

Saturnina's days are filled with caring for her two tiny daughters, sixteen-month-old Angelica and four-month-old Rosa Vidalia. The little sisters are often dressed like boys, so desired are male children in this society. The family compound is divided into three distinct areas. The first is a walled yard where Angelica can safely crawl and Saturnina can protect her plants, flourishing in large tin cans, from marauding chickens.

The baby's cradle, a shallow wooden box suspended by thin ropes, was hung under the roof of the front porch near a large, black setting hen. In the second area is the family's well, where Saturnina washes dishes and does laundry. On the opposite side of the house is the third area, a compound for small animals and poultry where numerous fruit trees grow. Though used for family consumption, animals and fruit are also an important source of revenue and, when ready, are taken to market.

Saturnina Garcia had made efforts to prepare the family altar for observance of the Day of the Dead. The tiny bedroom, where the altar was located, had been dismantled. Furniture, clothing, her husband's guitar, cowboy boots, tools, the couple's bed, the cradle, and all the paraphernalia women deem essential — combs, sashes, ribbons, beads, barrettes, string, needles and thread — had been transferred to the only other room in the house, the kitchen, the pile so large it buried the stove. Saturnina's veil, the one used on two of the most important occasions of her life, First Communion and her wedding, now served as a tablecloth for the altar.

Flores de muerto had been gathered and arranged in a metal pitcher, and two statues of saints and a holy picture in a red frame had been borrowed from a neighbor for the occasion. A *veladora* (votive candle), placed in a glass jar filled with kernels of corn to hold it straight, was lit in honor of the spirits of the family dead, who would come to visit that night. The altar preparations completed, Saturnina, dressed in a new *corte* and sweater, was ready for photographs. Her little daughters, however, were not; they howled throughout our time together, not mollified even by lollipops. Saturnina, calm and unfazed by the protestations of her little girls, focused on the photographs to come, the recording of this important occasion.

Teresa Culajay

It was a long, hot walk in the dry season to the house of Teresa Culajay. The cornstalks in the family *milpas* lay stricken, their growing finished, the last ears picked and stored. As I approached her house, I heard the sounds of daily life: the busy bustle of hens and their chicks, the grunts of pigs, the lowing of a calf, children playing; a soft feathering of wood smoke from the chimney curled above the roof of her house. Soon I passed an immense sow in advanced pregnancy protected from evil spirits by a colorful striped collar that Teresa had wound around the animal's neck, and I reached the house gate at last.

Teresa's first husband was killed here in Candelaria during the civil war, leaving her alone to raise their only child, a son, Miguel. Teresa, however, was fortunate enough to remarry several years later, at a time when there were many widows and a dearth of men to marry them. She and her second husband, Reyes Salazar, have produced five little daughters.

By not producing more sons they have placed the burden of helping the family onto Miguel, Teresa's oldest child. This illustrates why children are often unable to complete even the most basic education. That Miguel is highly capable, possessed of unusual intelligence and love for his studies, will not alleviate the family's need for his help.

Teresa, in her relaxed, easy manner, is a generous woman with a good sense of humor. She takes pride and pleasure in her family, their house, and their livestock. She had created an arbor of *güisquil* in a singular fashion, the large leaves resembling grape leaves covering the bamboo trellis over the porch. The *güisquiles*, which Teresa gave her children to eat throughout the day, are used as a filler in stews or baked like potatoes but have little nutritional value. It was disconcerting to discover that Teresa's children, who ate heartily the day of my visit, fell in the "malnourished" range of the PAVA growth charts. It is particularly difficult to realize

that little girls here are underfed, mainly because their beautiful traditional clothing conceals the real condition of their bodies, distracts the eye from the truth of their health. It is only when they are undressed and weighed that their true condition is apparent.

The family's house is divided into two distinct buildings, as is customary here: the first houses a generous-sized kitchen with a small section partitioned off in one corner serving as the family bedroom—two beds for seven people. The second serves as a corncrib and general storehouse, soon to be home, too, for a litter of black piglets from the great, collared sow. As the next harvest is still many months away, the corncrib is sparsely but neatly organized. Every cob is carefully placed and stored in its protective husk, stacked side by side, row on top of row. As the corn stacks diminish, expectancy rises for the next harvest to be abundant, to replenish the supply needed to allow Teresa's family to survive for one more year.

Zoila Camey

∧∧∧∧∧∧∧∧∧∧∧∧

When Zoila Camey spoke of her childhood, one of poignant loss, she said she had been born "a natural child"; she looked hard at me to make sure I understood the meaning of her words—that she was illegitimate. In 1976, when Zoila was ten years old, her mother died in the earthquake that killed more than 27,000 people in Guatemala. Zoila, orphaned and without any siblings, was raised by her maternal grandmother, who today is too ill and arthritic to participate in family photographs.

In 1982, at the height of the civil war, fifteen-year-old Zoila and seventeen-year-old Jose Cruz Bar were married. Both were born in Candelaria, and each had attended school for two years. Today they have three children—two sons and one daughter—all with high ratings on the PAVA growth charts. Zoila, who has had two miscarriages, feels no desire to limit the number of children she will have in the future; she says it "depends entirely on God."

More than traditional weaving, Zoila loves to sew. She showed me a blouse she had made for her daughter, three-year-old Delmis Somara, using an ancient, secondhand treadle machine bought recently for her by her husband. After making the blouse, she trimmed the neck and armholes with a crocheted border, in the tradition of women's blouses in this area, and embroidered large four-petaled flowers of bright, warm colors on the front. Owning a sewing machine, like owning a cow or a bicycle, is a sign of prosperity.

As lunchtime neared and her seven-year-old son returned from school, Zoila was disappointed that her husband did not return home too, as was his daily custom. For Zoila, this disappointment was particularly poignant. Having known so little family life as a child, she had worked hard to create her own family and wanted the photographs to prove it; with her husband missing, the photographs would be incomplete. Now she would not be able to show the world that she, too, was a member of a real family unit—her own.

———————

Glossary

a

atol — a nourishing drink made of powdered soybeans

b

bombas — explosives, louder than fire-crackers, used for celebrations

c

Cakchiquel — one of the four dominant tribes of the ancient Maya

calla lily — wild lily that proliferates in marshy areas during the rainy season

capitana — position of sacred honor and responsibility for women in the community

chilacayote — member of the squash family used in soups and sweets

chilco — wildflower of the fuschia family believed to bring good luck to a household

Chimaltenango — the department in which Candelaria is located

comal — flat clay dish used for cooking tortillas

Comité — male governing body of elected officials in a community

compañera — companion, friend

corona — crown, coronet

corte — traditional skirt made by wrapping a rectangular length of fabric around the body

f

finca — farm, property

flores de muerto — wild marigold that grows in abundance at the end of the rainy season in October, when the Day of the Dead and All Saints Day are celebrated; used to decorate houses and graves

frijoles — beans

h

huipil — loose-fitting blouse

m

manzana — a measure of land roughly equivalent to a city block

masa — dough made of cornmeal

mazorca de semilla — the finest ears of corn chosen from the harvest as seed for the next planting

metate — stone, usually volcanic, with a concave upper surface used for grinding or pulping seeds and vegetables; used primarily for rolling dough to make tortillas

milpa — cornfield

p

PAVA — Programa de Ayuda para los Vecinos del Altiplano (Program of Help for the Neighbors of the Highlands), the development group based in Chimalte-nango for which the author worked and through which she met the Women of Candelaria

pueblo — town, village

q

querencia — home, attachment to one's home, or a feeling of being at home

quetzales — Guatemalan currency named after an exotic bird, still in existence and highly prized by the ancient Maya

r

rebozo — long, narrow stole or shawl

s

sacate — bladed grass used for fodder

salvia — sage

San Martin Jilotepeque — the nearest large town to Candelaria and site of the marketplace

santos — saints

stelae — stone monuments of the ancient Maya, usually covered with bas-relief carvings

t

tinaja — large jar for carrying water; in the past made of earthenware, now made of plastic

v

veladora — small votive candle lit for religious purposes